MW01537311

THIS JOURNAL
Belongs To:

_____

_____

IMPORTANT Contacts

NAME & ADDRESS

NAME & ADDRESS

NAME & ADDRESS

NAME & ADDRESS

NAME & ADDRESS

NAME & ADDRESS

NAME & ADDRESS

NAME & ADDRESS

Emergency
CONTACT INFORMATION

POLICE DEPARTMENT

AMBULANCE SERVICES

MOM'S CELL NUMBER

SCHOOL

NEIGHBORS

RELATIVES

FIRE DEPARTMENT

POISON CONTROL

DAD'S CELL NUMBER

FAMILY DOCTOR

DENTIST

VETERINARIAN

OTHER

OTHER IMPORTANT INFORMATION

IMPORTANT CONTACTS

NAME & ADDRESS

NAME & ADDRESS

NAME & ADDRESS

NAME & ADDRESS

NAME & ADDRESS

NAME & ADDRESS

NAME & ADDRESS

NAME & ADDRESS

twenty 20

January

S	M	T	W	T	F	S
			1	2	3	4
5	6	7	8	9	10	11
12	13	14	15	16	17	18
19	20	21	22	23	24	25
26	27	28	29	30	31	

February

S	M	T	W	T	F	S
						1
2	3	4	5	6	7	8
9	10	11	12	13	14	15
16	17	18	19	20	21	22
23	24	25	26	27	28	29

March

S	M	T	W	T	F	S
1	2	3	4	5	6	7
8	9	10	11	12	13	14
15	16	17	18	19	20	21
22	23	24	25	26	27	28
29	30	31				

April

S	M	T	W	T	F	S
			1	2	3	4
5	6	7	8	9	10	11
12	13	14	15	16	17	18
19	20	21	22	23	24	25
26	27	28	29	30		

May

S	M	T	W	T	F	S
					1	2
3	4	5	6	7	8	9
10	11	12	13	14	15	16
17	18	19	20	21	22	23
24	25	26	27	28	29	30
31						

June

S	M	T	W	T	F	S
	1	2	3	4	5	6
7	8	9	10	11	12	13
14	15	16	17	18	19	20
21	22	23	24	25	26	27
28	29	30				

July

S	M	T	W	T	F	S
			1	2	3	4
5	6	7	8	9	10	11
12	13	14	15	16	17	18
19	20	21	22	23	24	25
26	27	28	29	30	31	

August

S	M	T	W	T	F	S
						1
2	3	4	5	6	7	8
9	10	11	12	13	14	15
16	17	18	19	20	21	22
23	24	25	26	27	28	29
30	31					

September

S	M	T	W	T	F	S
		1	2	3	4	5
6	7	8	9	10	11	12
13	14	15	16	17	18	19
20	21	22	23	24	25	26
27	28	29	30			

October

S	M	T	W	T	F	S
				1	2	3
4	5	6	7	8	9	10
11	12	13	14	15	16	17
18	19	20	21	22	23	24
25	26	27	28	29	30	31

November

S	M	T	W	T	F	S
1	2	3	4	5	6	7
8	9	10	11	12	13	14
15	16	17	18	19	20	21
22	23	24	25	26	27	28
29	30					

December

S	M	T	W	T	F	S
		1	2	3	4	5
6	7	8	9	10	11	12
13	14	15	16	17	18	19
20	21	22	23	24	25	26
27	28	29	30	31		

HOUSEHOLD Contacts

CONTRACTORS

REPAIR MAN

CLEANING SERVICES

SNOW REMOVAL SERVICES

LANDSCAPING SERVICES

GARBAGE & RECYCLING

BABYSITTERS:

SCHOOLS:

NOTES:

WEBSITES & Passwords

WEBSITE URL:	USERNAME:	PASSWORD:

NOTES:

Family

BIRTHDAYS & ANNIVERSARIES

JANUARY	JULY
FEBRUARY	AUGUST
MARCH	SEPTEMBER
APRIL	OCTOBER
MAY	NOVEMBER
JUNE	DECEMBER

OTHER IMPORTANT DATES

SCHOOL Information

SCHOOL NAME: PRINCIPAL:

SCHOOL ADDRESS: PHONE NUMBERS:

BUS DRIVER INFORMATION: TEACHER & CLASSROOM INFO:

ALL ABOUT THE KIDS

CHILD:	TEACHER:	CLASSROOM:	ROOM #:
CHILD:	TEACHER:	CLASSROOM:	ROOM #:
CHILD:	TEACHER:	CLASSROOM:	ROOM #:

MEDICAL Information

FAMILY DOCTOR

FAMILY DENTIST

OPTOMETRIST

PEDIATRICIAN

VETERINARIAN

FAMILY INSURANCE INFORMATION

IMPORTANT INFORMATION

ALLERGIES

BLOOD TYPES

WHAT:

WHO:

NAME:

BLOOD TYPE:

SEASONAL Cleaning

WINTER

SPRING

SUMMER

FALL/AUTUMN

SEASONAL Cleaning

WINTER

SPRING

SUMMER

FALL/AUTUMN

MEALS FOR THE WEEK

Monday

Tuesday

Wednesday

Thursday

Friday

Saturday

Sunday

FAMILY MEAL Planner

WEEK OF:

MEALS	M:	T:	W:	T:	F:	S:	S:
BREAKFAST							
SNACK							
LUNCH							
SNACK							
DINNER							
SNACK							

SHOPPING Checklist

GROCERY Checklist

Produce

Meats

Dairy

Frozen

Desserts

Misc.

TO DO Checklist

MONDAY

- [ ]
- [ ]
- [ ]
- [ ]
- [ ]
- [ ]
- [ ]
- [ ]

TUESDAY

- [ ]
- [ ]
- [ ]
- [ ]
- [ ]
- [ ]
- [ ]
- [ ]

WEDNESDAY

- [ ]
- [ ]
- [ ]
- [ ]
- [ ]
- [ ]
- [ ]
- [ ]

THURSDAY

- [ ]
- [ ]
- [ ]
- [ ]
- [ ]
- [ ]
- [ ]
- [ ]

FRIDAY

- [ ]
- [ ]
- [ ]
- [ ]
- [ ]
- [ ]
- [ ]
- [ ]

SATURDAY

- [ ]
- [ ]
- [ ]
- [ ]
- [ ]
- [ ]
- [ ]
- [ ]

SUNDAY

- [ ]
- [ ]
- [ ]
- [ ]
- [ ]
- [ ]
- [ ]
- [ ]

MOM TIME!

HOUSEWORK Checklist

CLEANING

WEEKLY CLEANING TO DO LIST

MONTHLY CLEANING TO DO LIST

WEEKLY TASK Checklist

MONDAY

- [ ]
- [ ]
- [ ]
- [ ]
- [ ]
- [ ]
- [ ]
- [ ]

TUESDAY

- [ ]
- [ ]
- [ ]
- [ ]
- [ ]
- [ ]
- [ ]
- [ ]

WEDNESDAY

- [ ]
- [ ]
- [ ]
- [ ]
- [ ]
- [ ]
- [ ]
- [ ]

THURSDAY

- [ ]
- [ ]
- [ ]
- [ ]
- [ ]
- [ ]
- [ ]
- [ ]

FRIDAY

- [ ]
- [ ]
- [ ]
- [ ]
- [ ]
- [ ]
- [ ]
- [ ]

SATURDAY

- [ ]
- [ ]
- [ ]
- [ ]
- [ ]
- [ ]
- [ ]
- [ ]

SUNDAY

- [ ]
- [ ]
- [ ]
- [ ]
- [ ]
- [ ]
- [ ]
- [ ]

MOM TIME!

SELF CARE Checklist

SELF CARE LIST

MON:

TUES:

WED:

THUR:

FRI:

SAT:

SUN:

MY PERSONAL TO-DO LIST:

☐
☐
☐
☐
☐
☐
☐
☐
☐
☐
☐
☐
☐
☐
☐

REMINDERS

FROM MOM'S Kitchen

Recipe

| PREP TIME: | BAKE TIME: | SERVES: |

Ingredients

Directions

FROM MOM'S Kitchen

Recipe

| PREP TIME: | BAKE TIME: | SERVES: |

Ingredients

Directions

KIDS CHORE Chart

NAME:

CHORE:	M:	T:	W:	T:	F:	S:	S:

KIDS CHORE Chart

NAME:							

CHORE:	M:	T:	W:	T:	F:	S:	S:

KIDS CHORE Chart

NAME:

CHORE:	M:	T:	W:	T:	F:	S:	S:

MY PERSONAL Goals

MY WEEKLY GOALS

- ☐
- ☐
- ☐
- ☐
- ☐
- ☐
- ☐
- ☐
- ☐

MY MONTHLY GOALS

- ☐
- ☐
- ☐
- ☐
- ☐
- ☐
- ☐
- ☐

MY YEARLY GOALS

- ☐
- ☐
- ☐
- ☐
- ☐
- ☐
- ☐

TURN Dreams INTO Reality

TIME FRAME	MY GOALS	STEPS I'LL TAKE
6 MONTHS		
1 YEAR		
2 YEARS		
5 YEARS		

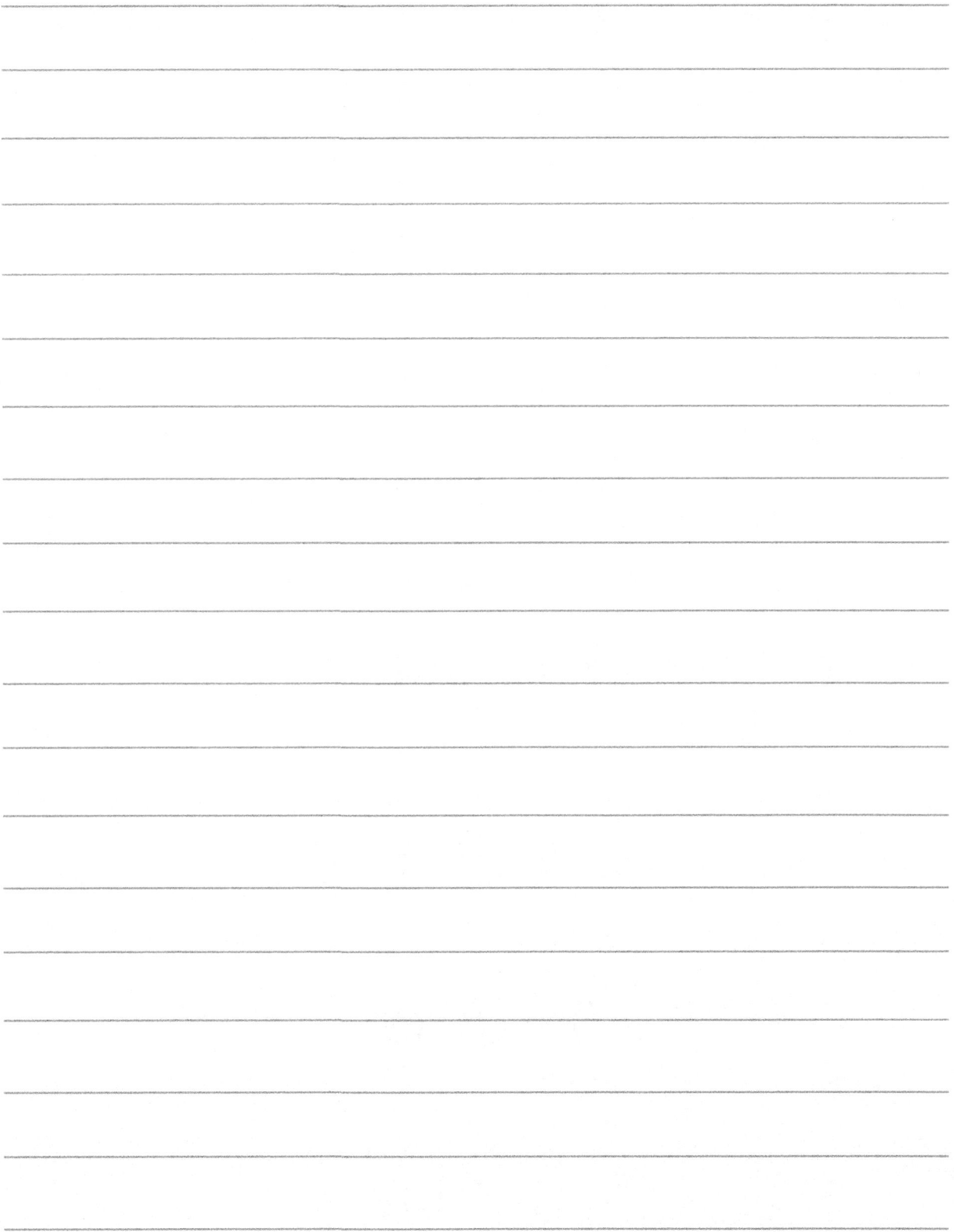

MEALS FOR THE WEEK

Monday

Tuesday

Wednesday

Thursday

Friday

Saturday

Sunday

FAMILY MEAL Planner

WEEK OF:

MEALS	M:	T:	W:	T:	F:	S:	S:
BREAKFAST							
SNACK							
LUNCH							
SNACK							
DINNER							
SNACK							

SHOPPING Checklist

GROCERY Checklist

Produce

Meats

Dairy

Frozen

Desserts

Misc.

TO DO Checklist

MONDAY

- [ ]
- [ ]
- [ ]
- [ ]
- [ ]
- [ ]
- [ ]

TUESDAY

- [ ]
- [ ]
- [ ]
- [ ]
- [ ]
- [ ]
- [ ]

WEDNESDAY

- [ ]
- [ ]
- [ ]
- [ ]
- [ ]
- [ ]
- [ ]

THURSDAY

- [ ]
- [ ]
- [ ]
- [ ]
- [ ]
- [ ]
- [ ]

FRIDAY

- [ ]
- [ ]
- [ ]
- [ ]
- [ ]
- [ ]
- [ ]

SATURDAY

- [ ]
- [ ]
- [ ]
- [ ]
- [ ]
- [ ]

SUNDAY

- [ ]
- [ ]
- [ ]
- [ ]
- [ ]
- [ ]
- [ ]

MOM TIME!

HOUSEWORK Checklist

CLEANING

WEEKLY CLEANING TO DO LIST

MONTHLY CLEANING TO DO LIST

WEEKLY TASK Checklist

MONDAY

- ☐
- ☐
- ☐
- ☐
- ☐
- ☐
- ☐
- ☐

TUESDAY

- ☐
- ☐
- ☐
- ☐
- ☐
- ☐
- ☐
- ☐

WEDNESDAY

- ☐
- ☐
- ☐
- ☐
- ☐
- ☐
- ☐
- ☐

THURSDAY

- ☐
- ☐
- ☐
- ☐
- ☐
- ☐
- ☐
- ☐

FRIDAY

- ☐
- ☐
- ☐
- ☐
- ☐
- ☐
- ☐
- ☐

SATURDAY

- ☐
- ☐
- ☐
- ☐
- ☐
- ☐
- ☐
- ☐

SUNDAY

- ☐
- ☐
- ☐
- ☐
- ☐
- ☐
- ☐
- ☐

MOM TIME!

SELF CARE Checklist

SELF CARE LIST

MON:

TUES:

WED:

THUR:

FRI:

SAT:

SUN:

REMINDERS

MY PERSONAL TO-DO LIST:

FROM MOM'S Kitchen

Recipe

PREP TIME:	BAKE TIME:	SERVES:

Ingredients

Directions

FROM MOM'S Kitchen

Recipe

PREP TIME:	BAKE TIME:	SERVES:

Ingredients

Directions

KIDS CHORE Chart

NAME:

CHORE:	M:	T:	W:	T:	F:	S:	S:

KIDS CHORE Chart

NAME:							

CHORE:	M:	T:	W:	T:	F:	S:	S:

KIDS CHORE Chart

NAME:

CHORE:	M:	T:	W:	T:	F:	S:	S:

MY PERSONAL Goals

MY WEEKLY GOALS

- [ ]
- [ ]
- [ ]
- [ ]
- [ ]
- [ ]
- [ ]
- [ ]
- [ ]

MY MONTHLY GOALS

- [ ]
- [ ]
- [ ]
- [ ]
- [ ]
- [ ]
- [ ]
- [ ]

MY YEARLY GOALS

- [ ]
- [ ]
- [ ]
- [ ]
- [ ]
- [ ]
- [ ]

- [ ]
- [ ]
- [ ]
- [ ]
- [ ]
- [ ]

TURN Dreams INTO Reality

TIME FRAME	MY GOALS	STEPS I'LL TAKE
6 MONTHS		
1 YEAR		
2 YEARS		
5 YEARS		

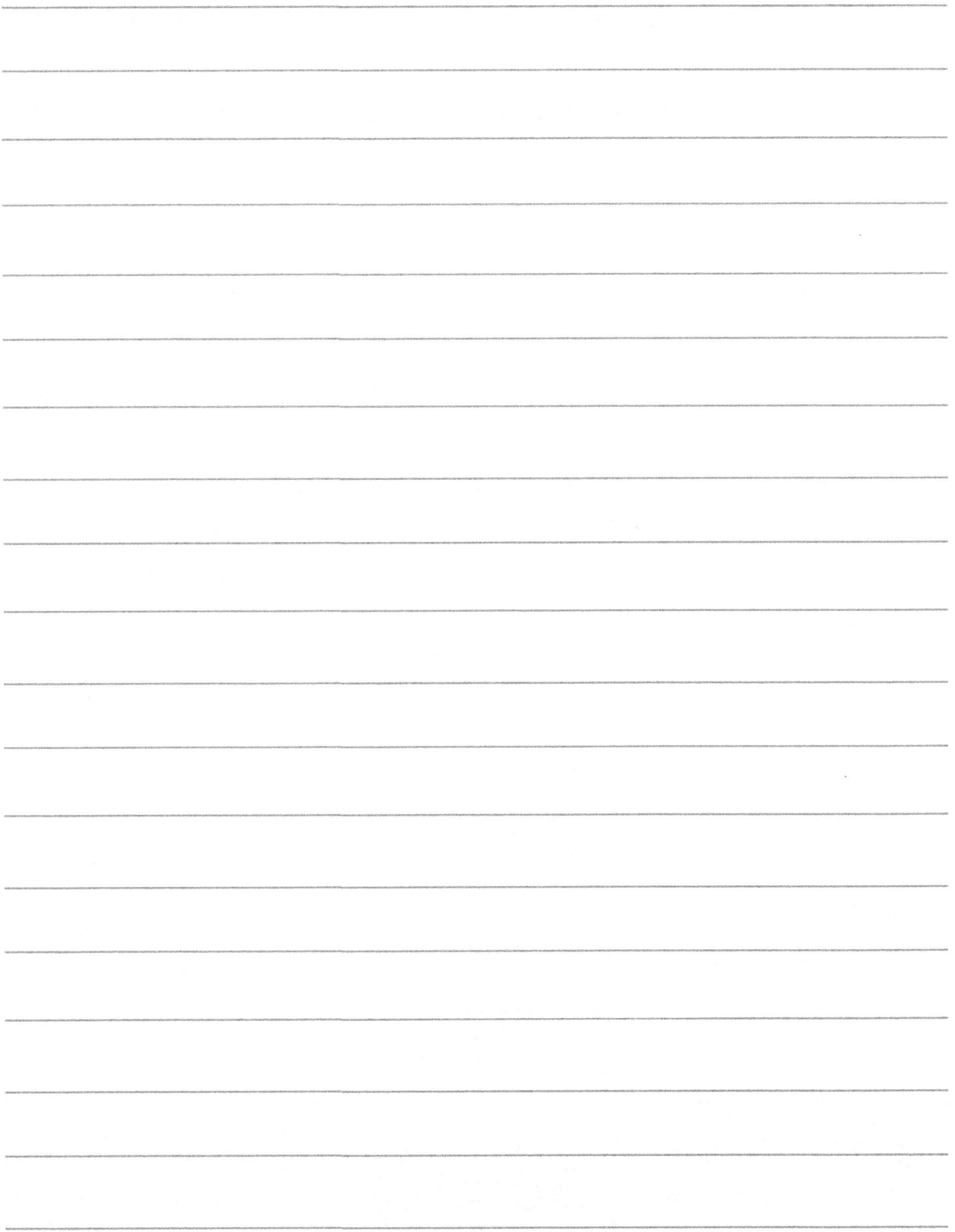

MEALS FOR THE WEEK

Monday

Tuesday

Wednesday

Thursday

Friday

Saturday

Sunday

FAMILY MEAL Planner

WEEK OF:

MEALS	M:	T:	W:	T:	F:	S:	S:
BREAKFAST							
SNACK							
LUNCH							
SNACK							
DINNER							
SNACK							

SHOPPING Checklist

GROCERY Checklist

Produce

Meats

Dairy

Frozen

Desserts

Misc.

TO DO Checklist

MONDAY

- [ ]
- [ ]
- [ ]
- [ ]
- [ ]
- [ ]
- [ ]
- [ ]

TUESDAY

- [ ]
- [ ]
- [ ]
- [ ]
- [ ]
- [ ]
- [ ]
- [ ]

WEDNESDAY

- [ ]
- [ ]
- [ ]
- [ ]
- [ ]
- [ ]
- [ ]

THURSDAY

- [ ]
- [ ]
- [ ]
- [ ]
- [ ]
- [ ]
- [ ]
- [ ]

FRIDAY

- [ ]
- [ ]
- [ ]
- [ ]
- [ ]
- [ ]
- [ ]

SATURDAY

- [ ]
- [ ]
- [ ]
- [ ]
- [ ]
- [ ]
- [ ]

SUNDAY

- [ ]
- [ ]
- [ ]
- [ ]
- [ ]
- [ ]
- [ ]
- [ ]

MOM TIME!

HOUSEWORK Checklist

CLEANING

WEEKLY CLEANING TO DO LIST

MONTHLY CLEANING TO DO LIST

WEEKLY TASK Checklist

MONDAY

- [ ]
- [ ]
- [ ]
- [ ]
- [ ]
- [ ]
- [ ]

TUESDAY

- [ ]
- [ ]
- [ ]
- [ ]
- [ ]
- [ ]
- [ ]

WEDNESDAY

- [ ]
- [ ]
- [ ]
- [ ]
- [ ]
- [ ]
- [ ]

THURSDAY

- [ ]
- [ ]
- [ ]
- [ ]
- [ ]
- [ ]
- [ ]

FRIDAY

- [ ]
- [ ]
- [ ]
- [ ]
- [ ]
- [ ]
- [ ]

SATURDAY

- [ ]
- [ ]
- [ ]
- [ ]
- [ ]
- [ ]
- [ ]

SUNDAY

- [ ]
- [ ]
- [ ]
- [ ]
- [ ]
- [ ]
- [ ]

MOM TIME!

SELF CARE Checklist

SELF CARE LIST

MON:

TUES:

WED:

THUR:

FRI:

SAT:

SUN:

MY PERSONAL TO-DO LIST:

☐
☐
☐
☐
☐
☐
☐
☐
☐
☐
☐
☐
☐
☐
☐

REMINDERS

FROM MOM'S Kitchen

Recipe

| PREP TIME: | BAKE TIME: | SERVES: |

Ingredients

Directions

FROM MOM'S Kitchen

Recipe

PREP TIME:

BAKE TIME:

SERVES:

Ingredients

Directions

KIDS CHORE Chart

NAME:

CHORE:	M:	T:	W:	T:	F:	S:	S:

KIDS CHORE Chart

NAME:							

CHORE:	M:	T:	W:	T:	F:	S:	S:

KIDS CHORE Chart

NAME:

CHORE:	M:	T:	W:	T:	F:	S:	S:

MY PERSONAL Goals

MY WEEKLY GOALS

MY MONTHLY GOALS

MY YEARLY GOALS

TURN Dreams INTO Reality

TIME FRAME	MY GOALS	STEPS I'LL TAKE
6 MONTHS		
1 YEAR		
2 YEARS		
5 YEARS		

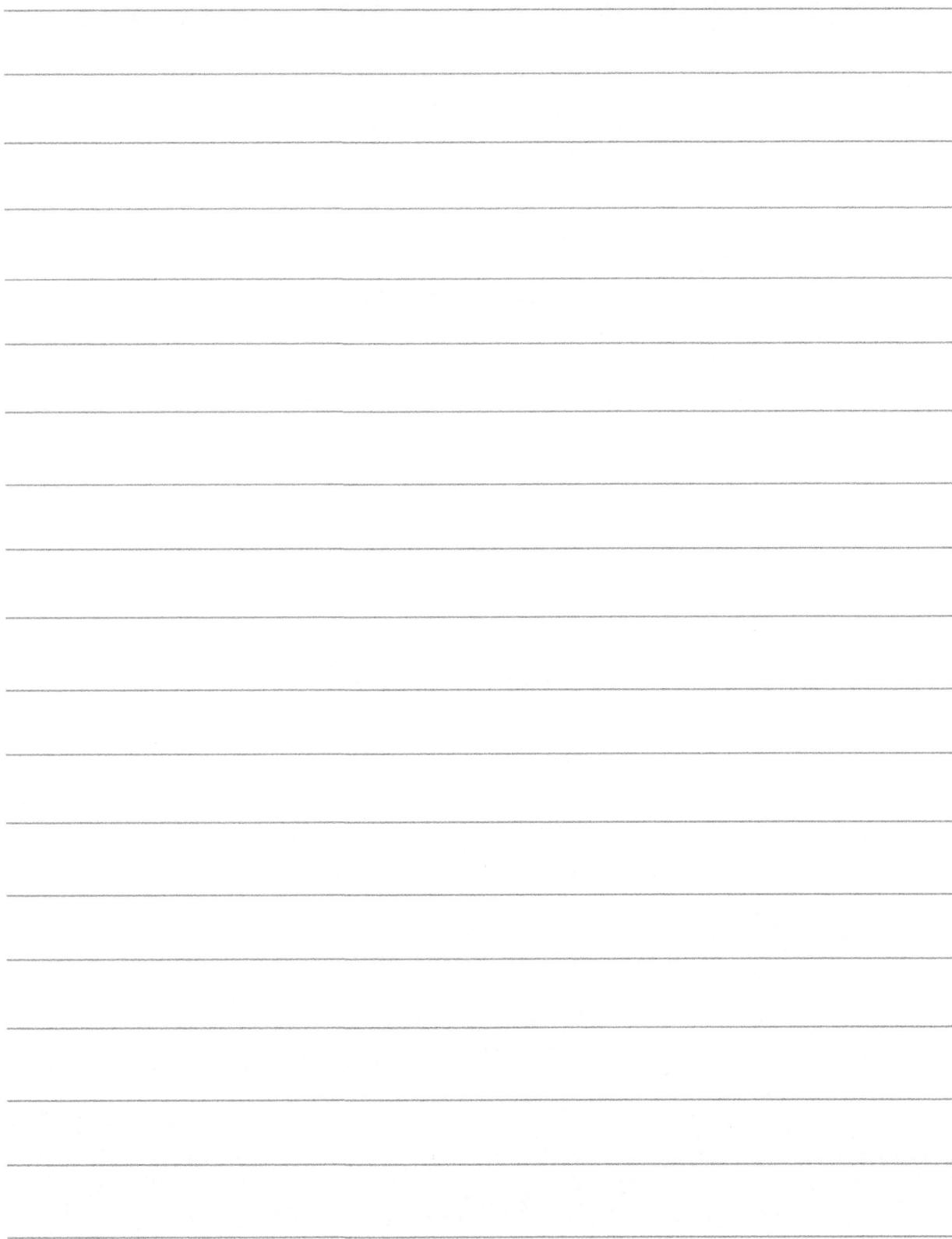

MEALS FOR THE WEEK

Monday

Tuesday

Wednesday

Thursday

Friday

Saturday

Sunday

FAMILY MEAL Planner

WEEK OF:

MEALS	M:	T:	W:	T:	F:	S:	S:
BREAKFAST							
SNACK							
LUNCH							
SNACK							
DINNER							
SNACK							

SHOPPING Checklist

GROCERY **Checklist**

Produce

Meats

Dairy

Frozen

Desserts

Misc.

TO DO Checklist

MONDAY

- [ ]
- [ ]
- [ ]
- [ ]
- [ ]
- [ ]
- [ ]
- [ ]

TUESDAY

- [ ]
- [ ]
- [ ]
- [ ]
- [ ]
- [ ]
- [ ]
- [ ]

WEDNESDAY

- [ ]
- [ ]
- [ ]
- [ ]
- [ ]
- [ ]
- [ ]
- [ ]

THURSDAY

- [ ]
- [ ]
- [ ]
- [ ]
- [ ]
- [ ]
- [ ]

FRIDAY

- [ ]
- [ ]
- [ ]
- [ ]
- [ ]
- [ ]
- [ ]

SATURDAY

- [ ]
- [ ]
- [ ]
- [ ]
- [ ]
- [ ]
- [ ]

SUNDAY

- [ ]
- [ ]
- [ ]
- [ ]
- [ ]
- [ ]
- [ ]
- [ ]

MOM TIME!

HOUSEWORK Checklist

CLEANING

WEEKLY CLEANING TO DO LIST

MONTHLY CLEANING TO DO LIST

WEEKLY TASK Checklist

MONDAY

- [ ]
- [ ]
- [ ]
- [ ]
- [ ]
- [ ]
- [ ]

TUESDAY

- [ ]
- [ ]
- [ ]
- [ ]
- [ ]
- [ ]
- [ ]

WEDNESDAY

- [ ]
- [ ]
- [ ]
- [ ]
- [ ]
- [ ]
- [ ]

THURSDAY

- [ ]
- [ ]
- [ ]
- [ ]
- [ ]
- [ ]
- [ ]

FRIDAY

- [ ]
- [ ]
- [ ]
- [ ]
- [ ]
- [ ]
- [ ]

SATURDAY

- [ ]
- [ ]
- [ ]
- [ ]
- [ ]
- [ ]
- [ ]

SUNDAY

- [ ]
- [ ]
- [ ]
- [ ]
- [ ]
- [ ]
- [ ]

MOM TIME!

SELF CARE Checklist

SELF CARE LIST
MON:
TUES:
WED:
THUR:
FRI:
SAT:
SUN:

MY PERSONAL TO-DO LIST:

- ☐
- ☐
- ☐
- ☐
- ☐
- ☐
- ☐
- ☐
- ☐
- ☐
- ☐
- ☐
- ☐
- ☐
- ☐

REMINDERS

FROM MOM'S Kitchen

Recipe

| PREP TIME: | BAKE TIME: | SERVES: |

Ingredients

Directions

FROM MOM'S Kitchen

Recipe

PREP TIME:

BAKE TIME:

SERVES:

Ingredients

Directions

KIDS CHORE Chart

NAME:

CHORE:	M:	T:	W:	T:	F:	S:	S:

KIDS CHORE Chart

NAME:

CHORE:	M:	T:	W:	T:	F:	S:	S:

KIDS CHORE Chart

NAME:

CHORE:	M:	T:	W:	T:	F:	S:	S:

MY PERSONAL Goals

MY WEEKLY GOALS

- [ ]
- [ ]
- [ ]
- [ ]
- [ ]
- [ ]
- [ ]
- [ ]
- [ ]

MY MONTHLY GOALS

- [ ]
- [ ]
- [ ]
- [ ]
- [ ]
- [ ]
- [ ]
- [ ]

MY YEARLY GOALS

- [ ]
- [ ]
- [ ]
- [ ]
- [ ]
- [ ]
- [ ]

- [ ]
- [ ]
- [ ]
- [ ]
- [ ]
- [ ]
- [ ]

TURN Dreams INTO Reality

TIME FRAME	MY GOALS	STEPS I'LL TAKE
6 MONTHS		
1 YEAR		
2 YEARS		
5 YEARS		

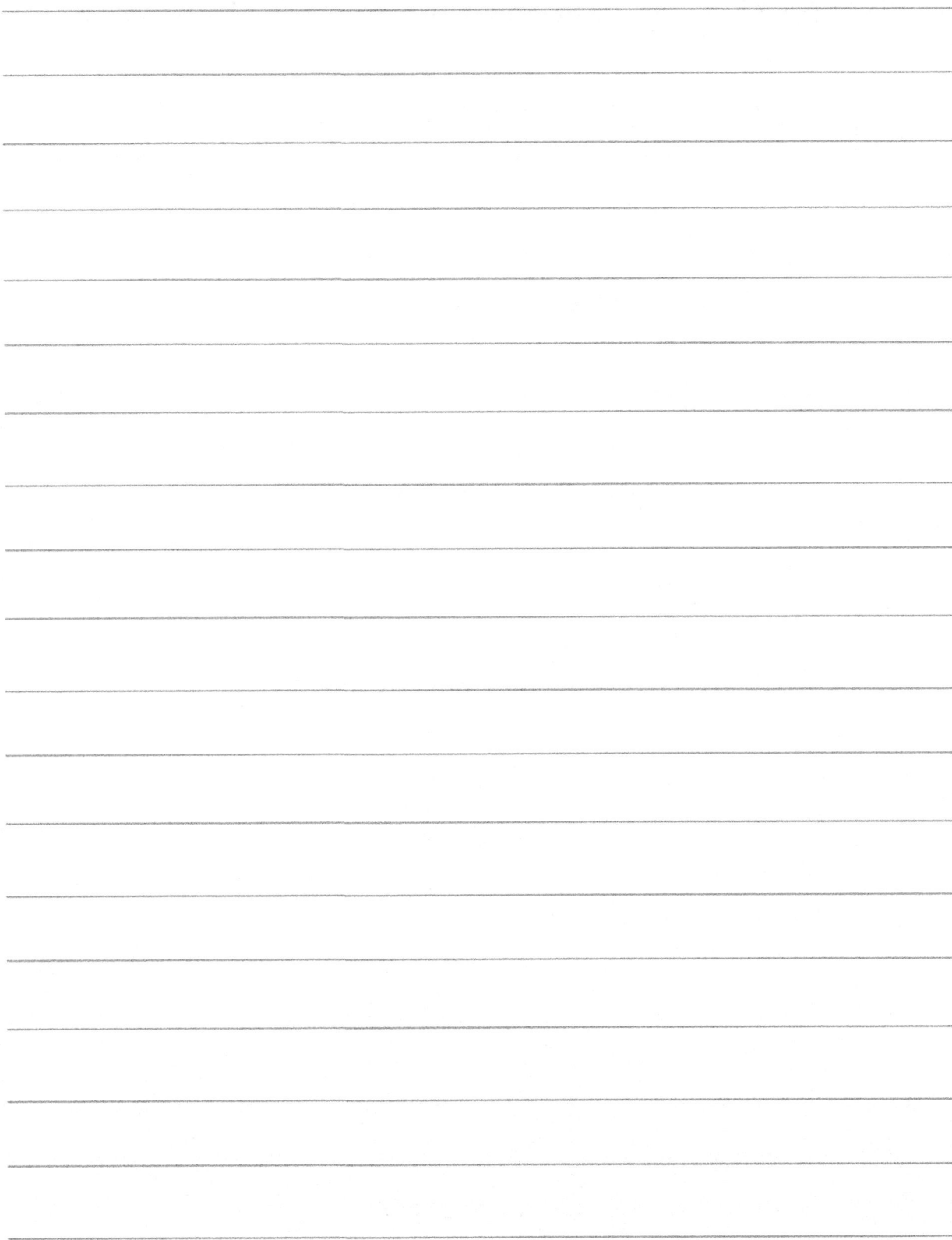

MEALS FOR THE WEEK

Monday

Tuesday

Wednesday

Thursday

Friday

Saturday

Sunday

FAMILY MEAL Planner

WEEK OF:

MEALS	M:	T:	W:	T:	F:	S:	S:
BREAKFAST							
SNACK							
LUNCH							
SNACK							
DINNER							
SNACK							

SHOPPING Checklist

GROCERY **Checklist**

Produce

Meats

Dairy

Frozen

Desserts

Misc.

TO DO Checklist

MONDAY
- [ ]
- [ ]
- [ ]
- [ ]
- [ ]
- [ ]
- [ ]
- [ ]

TUESDAY
- [ ]
- [ ]
- [ ]
- [ ]
- [ ]
- [ ]
- [ ]
- [ ]

WEDNESDAY
- [ ]
- [ ]
- [ ]
- [ ]
- [ ]
- [ ]
- [ ]
- [ ]

THURSDAY
- [ ]
- [ ]
- [ ]
- [ ]
- [ ]
- [ ]
- [ ]
- [ ]

FRIDAY
- [ ]
- [ ]
- [ ]
- [ ]
- [ ]
- [ ]
- [ ]
- [ ]

SATURDAY
- [ ]
- [ ]
- [ ]
- [ ]
- [ ]
- [ ]
- [ ]
- [ ]

SUNDAY
- [ ]
- [ ]
- [ ]
- [ ]
- [ ]
- [ ]
- [ ]
- [ ]

MOM TIME!

HOUSEWORK Checklist

CLEANING

WEEKLY CLEANING TO DO LIST

MONTHLY CLEANING TO DO LIST

WEEKLY TASK Checklist

MONDAY

- [ ]
- [ ]
- [ ]
- [ ]
- [ ]
- [ ]
- [ ]

TUESDAY

- [ ]
- [ ]
- [ ]
- [ ]
- [ ]
- [ ]
- [ ]

WEDNESDAY

- [ ]
- [ ]
- [ ]
- [ ]
- [ ]
- [ ]
- [ ]

THURSDAY

- [ ]
- [ ]
- [ ]
- [ ]
- [ ]
- [ ]
- [ ]

FRIDAY

- [ ]
- [ ]
- [ ]
- [ ]
- [ ]
- [ ]

SATURDAY

- [ ]
- [ ]
- [ ]
- [ ]
- [ ]
- [ ]

SUNDAY

- [ ]
- [ ]
- [ ]
- [ ]
- [ ]
- [ ]
- [ ]

MOM TIME!

SELF CARE Checklist

SELF CARE LIST

MON:

TUES:

WED:

THUR:

FRI:

SAT:

SUN:

REMINDERS

MY PERSONAL TO-DO LIST:

☐
☐
☐
☐
☐
☐
☐
☐
☐
☐
☐
☐
☐
☐
☐
☐

FROM MOM'S Kitchen

Recipe

PREP TIME:	BAKE TIME:	SERVES:

Ingredients

Directions

FROM MOM'S Kitchen

Recipe

PREP TIME:

BAKE TIME:

SERVES:

Ingredients

Directions

KIDS CHORE Chart

NAME:

CHORE:	M:	T:	W:	T:	F:	S:	S:

KIDS CHORE Chart

NAME:

CHORE:	M:	T:	W:	T:	F:	S:	S:

KIDS CHORE Chart

NAME:

CHORE:	M:	T:	W:	T:	F:	S:	S:

MY PERSONAL Goals

MY WEEKLY GOALS

MY MONTHLY GOALS

MY YEARLY GOALS

TURN Dreams INTO Reality

TIME FRAME	MY GOALS	STEPS I'LL TAKE
6 MONTHS		
1 YEAR		
2 YEARS		
5 YEARS		

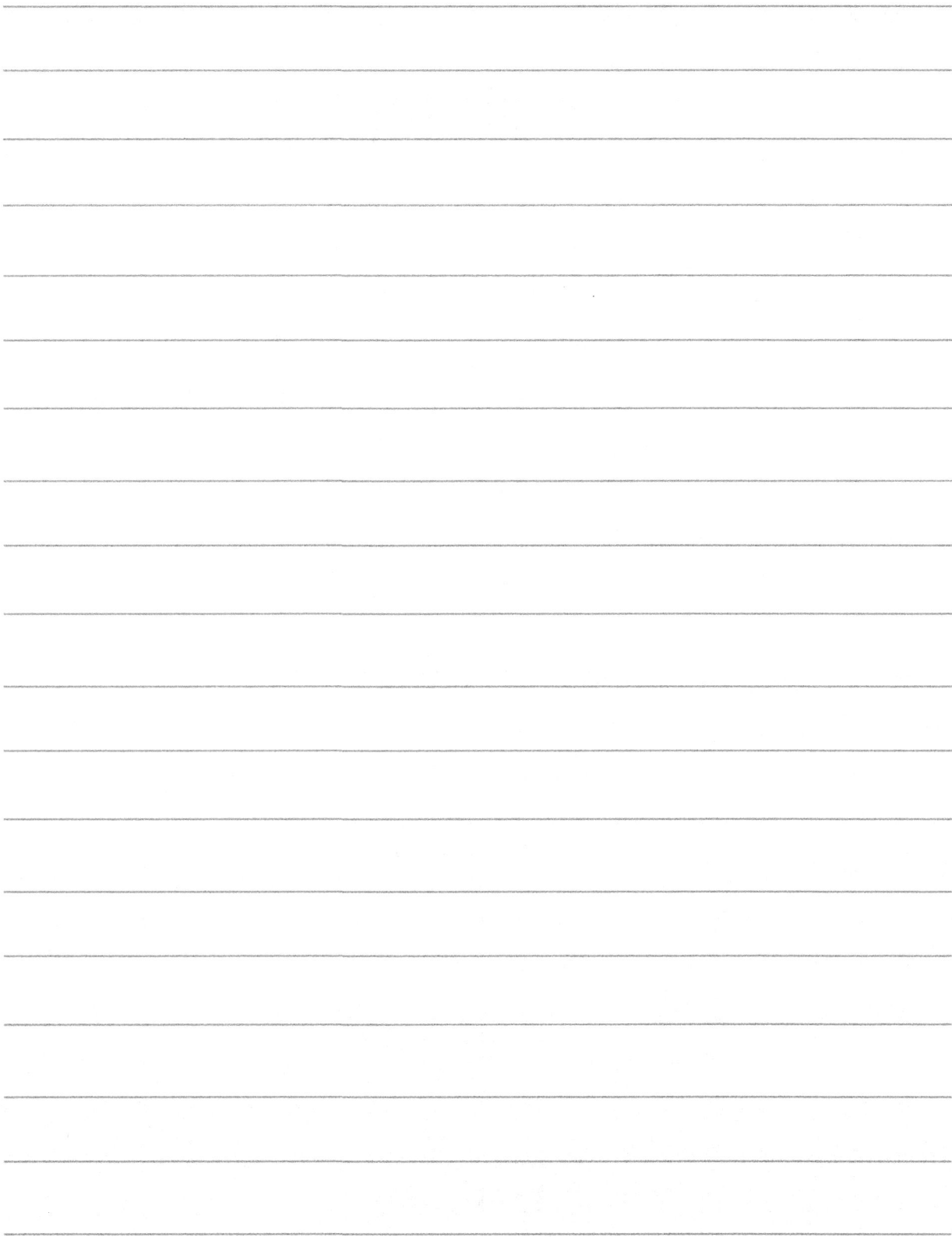

MEALS FOR THE WEEK

Monday

Tuesday

Wednesday

Thursday

Friday

Saturday

Sunday

FAMILY MEAL Planner

WEEK OF:

MEALS	M:	T:	W:	T:	F:	S:	S:
BREAKFAST							
SNACK							
LUNCH							
SNACK							
DINNER							
SNACK							

SHOPPING Checklist

GROCERY **Checklist**

Produce

Meats

Dairy

Frozen

Desserts

Misc.

TO DO Checklist

MONDAY

- [ ]
- [ ]
- [ ]
- [ ]
- [ ]
- [ ]
- [ ]
- [ ]

TUESDAY

- [ ]
- [ ]
- [ ]
- [ ]
- [ ]
- [ ]
- [ ]
- [ ]

WEDNESDAY

- [ ]
- [ ]
- [ ]
- [ ]
- [ ]
- [ ]
- [ ]
- [ ]

THURSDAY

- [ ]
- [ ]
- [ ]
- [ ]
- [ ]
- [ ]
- [ ]
- [ ]

FRIDAY

- [ ]
- [ ]
- [ ]
- [ ]
- [ ]
- [ ]
- [ ]
- [ ]

SATURDAY

- [ ]
- [ ]
- [ ]
- [ ]
- [ ]
- [ ]
- [ ]

SUNDAY

- [ ]
- [ ]
- [ ]
- [ ]
- [ ]
- [ ]
- [ ]
- [ ]

MOM TIME!

HOUSEWORK Checklist

CLEANING

WEEKLY CLEANING TO DO LIST

MONTHLY CLEANING TO DO LIST

WEEKLY TASK Checklist

MONDAY

- [ ]
- [ ]
- [ ]
- [ ]
- [ ]
- [ ]
- [ ]
- [ ]

TUESDAY

- [ ]
- [ ]
- [ ]
- [ ]
- [ ]
- [ ]
- [ ]
- [ ]

WEDNESDAY

- [ ]
- [ ]
- [ ]
- [ ]
- [ ]
- [ ]
- [ ]
- [ ]

THURSDAY

- [ ]
- [ ]
- [ ]
- [ ]
- [ ]
- [ ]
- [ ]
- [ ]

FRIDAY

- [ ]
- [ ]
- [ ]
- [ ]
- [ ]
- [ ]
- [ ]
- [ ]

SATURDAY

- [ ]
- [ ]
- [ ]
- [ ]
- [ ]
- [ ]
- [ ]
- [ ]

SUNDAY

- [ ]
- [ ]
- [ ]
- [ ]
- [ ]
- [ ]
- [ ]
- [ ]

MOM TIME!

SELF CARE Checklist

SELF CARE LIST	MY PERSONAL TO-DO LIST:
MON:	☐
TUES:	☐
WED:	☐
THUR:	☐
FRI:	☐
SAT:	☐
SUN:	☐

REMINDERS

FROM MOM'S Kitchen

Recipe

PREP TIME:	BAKE TIME:	SERVES:

Ingredients

Directions

FROM MOM'S Kitchen

Recipe

| PREP TIME: | BAKE TIME: | SERVES: |

Ingredients

Directions

KIDS CHORE Chart

NAME:

CHORE:	M:	T:	W:	T:	F:	S:	S:

KIDS CHORE Chart

NAME:							

CHORE:	M:	T:	W:	T:	F:	S:	S:

KIDS CHORE Chart

NAME:

CHORE:	M:	T:	W:	T:	F:	S:	S:

MY PERSONAL Goals

MY WEEKLY GOALS

MY MONTHLY GOALS

MY YEARLY GOALS

TURN Dreams INTO Reality

TIME FRAME	MY GOALS	STEPS I'LL TAKE
6 MONTHS		
1 YEAR		
2 YEARS		
5 YEARS		

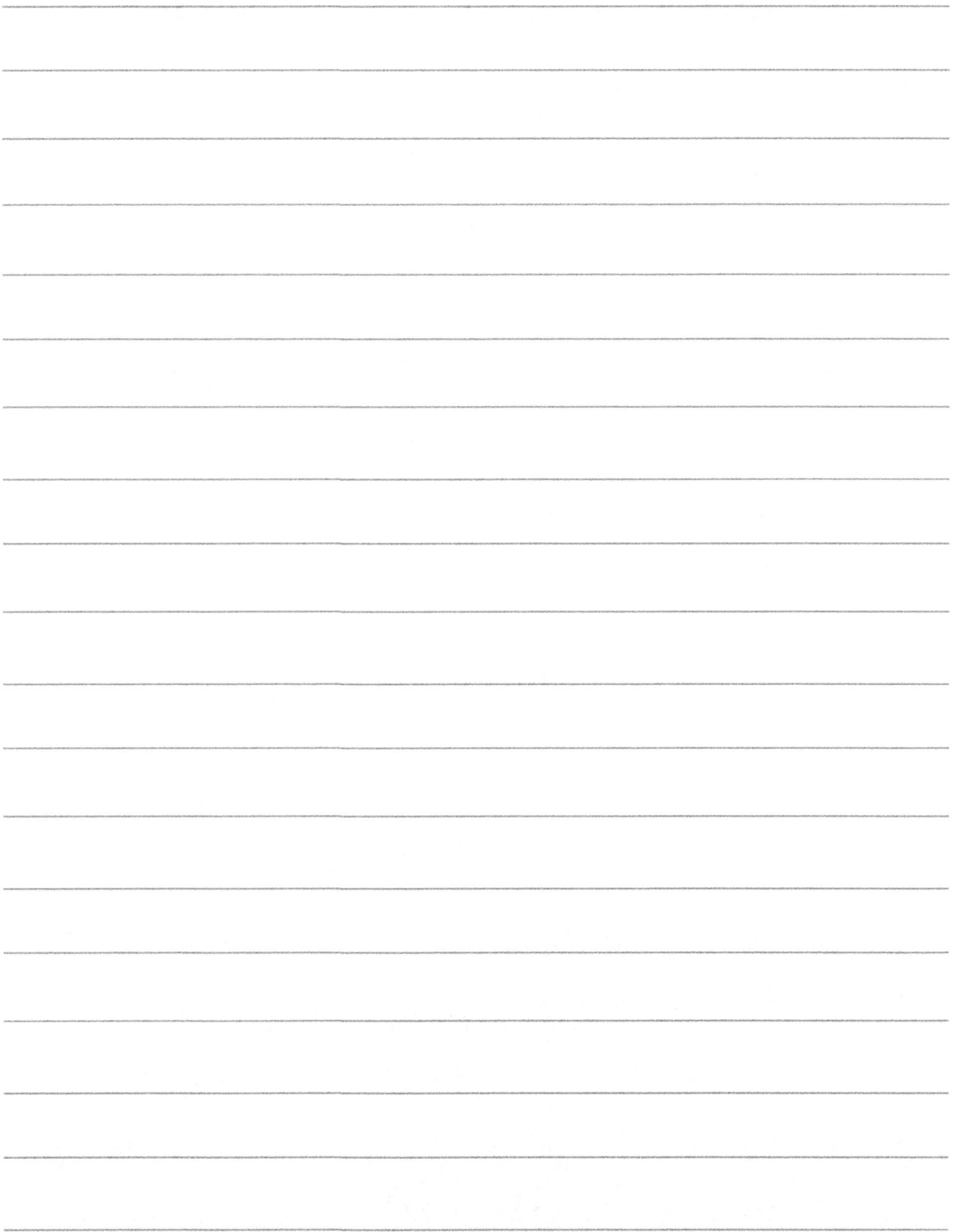

MEALS FOR THE WEEK

Monday

Tuesday

Wednesday

Thursday

Friday

Saturday

Sunday

FAMILY MEAL Planner

WEEK OF:

MEALS	M:	T:	W:	T:	F:	S:	S:
BREAKFAST							
SNACK							
LUNCH							
SNACK							
DINNER							
SNACK							

SHOPPING Checklist

GROCERY Checklist

Produce

Meats

Dairy

Frozen

Desserts

Misc.

TO DO Checklist

MONDAY

- [ ]
- [ ]
- [ ]
- [ ]
- [ ]
- [ ]
- [ ]
- [ ]

TUESDAY

- [ ]
- [ ]
- [ ]
- [ ]
- [ ]
- [ ]
- [ ]
- [ ]

WEDNESDAY

- [ ]
- [ ]
- [ ]
- [ ]
- [ ]
- [ ]
- [ ]
- [ ]

THURSDAY

- [ ]
- [ ]
- [ ]
- [ ]
- [ ]
- [ ]
- [ ]
- [ ]

FRIDAY

- [ ]
- [ ]
- [ ]
- [ ]
- [ ]
- [ ]
- [ ]
- [ ]

SATURDAY

- [ ]
- [ ]
- [ ]
- [ ]
- [ ]
- [ ]
- [ ]
- [ ]

SUNDAY

- [ ]
- [ ]
- [ ]
- [ ]
- [ ]
- [ ]
- [ ]

MOM TIME!

HOUSEWORK Checklist

CLEANING

WEEKLY CLEANING TO DO LIST

MONTHLY CLEANING TO DO LIST

WEEKLY TASK Checklist

MONDAY

- [ ]
- [ ]
- [ ]
- [ ]
- [ ]
- [ ]
- [ ]
- [ ]

TUESDAY

- [ ]
- [ ]
- [ ]
- [ ]
- [ ]
- [ ]
- [ ]
- [ ]

WEDNESDAY

- [ ]
- [ ]
- [ ]
- [ ]
- [ ]
- [ ]
- [ ]

THURSDAY

- [ ]
- [ ]
- [ ]
- [ ]
- [ ]
- [ ]
- [ ]
- [ ]

FRIDAY

- [ ]
- [ ]
- [ ]
- [ ]
- [ ]
- [ ]
- [ ]

SATURDAY

- [ ]
- [ ]
- [ ]
- [ ]
- [ ]
- [ ]
- [ ]

SUNDAY

- [ ]
- [ ]
- [ ]
- [ ]
- [ ]
- [ ]
- [ ]
- [ ]

MOM TIME!

SELF CARE Checklist

SELF CARE LIST	MY PERSONAL TO-DO LIST:
MON:	
TUES:	
WED:	
THUR:	
FRI:	
SAT:	
SUN:	

REMINDERS

FROM MOM'S Kitchen

Recipe

PREP TIME:	BAKE TIME:	SERVES:

Ingredients

Directions

FROM MOM'S Kitchen

Recipe

PREP TIME:

BAKE TIME:

SERVES:

Ingredients

Directions

KIDS CHORE Chart

NAME:

CHORE:	M:	T:	W:	T:	F:	S:	S:

KIDS CHORE Chart

NAME:

CHORE:	M:	T:	W:	T:	F:	S:	S:

KIDS CHORE Chart

NAME:

CHORE:	M:	T:	W:	T:	F:	S:	S:

MY PERSONAL Goals

MY WEEKLY GOALS

- [ ]
- [ ]
- [ ]
- [ ]
- [ ]
- [ ]
- [ ]
- [ ]
- [ ]

MY MONTHLY GOALS

- [ ]
- [ ]
- [ ]
- [ ]
- [ ]
- [ ]
- [ ]
- [ ]

MY YEARLY GOALS

- [ ]
- [ ]
- [ ]
- [ ]
- [ ]
- [ ]
- [ ]

TURN Dreams INTO Reality

TIME FRAME	MY GOALS	STEPS I'LL TAKE
6 MONTHS		
1 YEAR		
2 YEARS		
5 YEARS		

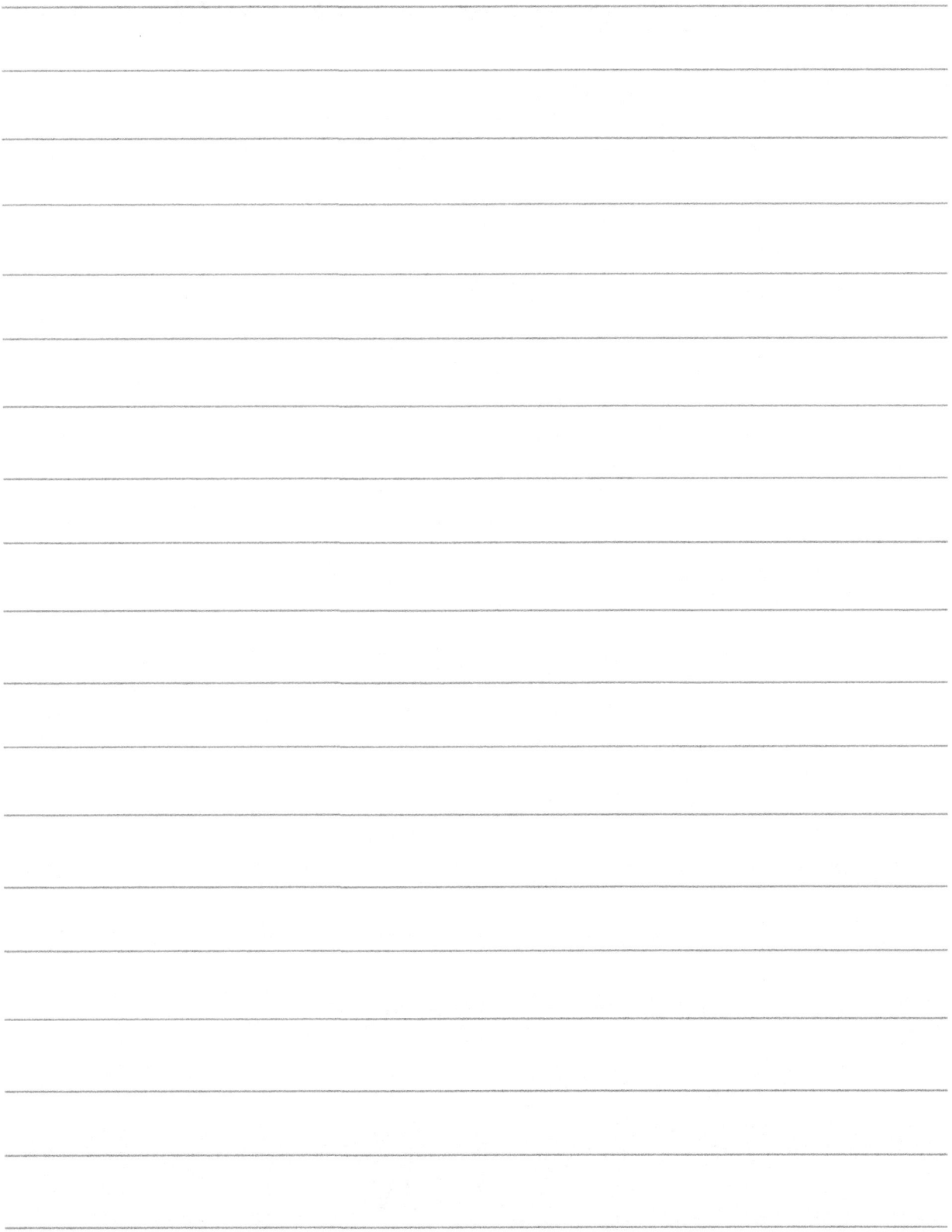

MEALS FOR THE WEEK

Monday

Tuesday

Wednesday

Thursday

Friday

Saturday

Sunday

FAMILY MEAL Planner

WEEK OF:

MEALS	M:	T:	W:	T:	F:	S:	S:
BREAKFAST							
SNACK							
LUNCH							
SNACK							
DINNER							
SNACK							

SHOPPING Checklist

GROCERY **Checklist**

Produce

Meats

Dairy

Frozen

Desserts

Misc.

TO DO Checklist

MONDAY

- [ ]
- [ ]
- [ ]
- [ ]
- [ ]
- [ ]
- [ ]
- [ ]

TUESDAY

- [ ]
- [ ]
- [ ]
- [ ]
- [ ]
- [ ]
- [ ]
- [ ]

WEDNESDAY

- [ ]
- [ ]
- [ ]
- [ ]
- [ ]
- [ ]
- [ ]
- [ ]

THURSDAY

- [ ]
- [ ]
- [ ]
- [ ]
- [ ]
- [ ]
- [ ]
- [ ]

FRIDAY

- [ ]
- [ ]
- [ ]
- [ ]
- [ ]
- [ ]
- [ ]
- [ ]

SATURDAY

- [ ]
- [ ]
- [ ]
- [ ]
- [ ]
- [ ]
- [ ]
- [ ]

SUNDAY

- [ ]
- [ ]
- [ ]
- [ ]
- [ ]
- [ ]
- [ ]
- [ ]

MOM TIME!

HOUSEWORK Checklist

CLEANING

WEEKLY CLEANING TO DO LIST

MONTHLY CLEANING TO DO LIST

WEEKLY TASK Checklist

MONDAY

- [ ]
- [ ]
- [ ]
- [ ]
- [ ]
- [ ]
- [ ]

TUESDAY

- [ ]
- [ ]
- [ ]
- [ ]
- [ ]
- [ ]
- [ ]

WEDNESDAY

- [ ]
- [ ]
- [ ]
- [ ]
- [ ]
- [ ]
- [ ]

THURSDAY

- [ ]
- [ ]
- [ ]
- [ ]
- [ ]
- [ ]
- [ ]

FRIDAY

- [ ]
- [ ]
- [ ]
- [ ]
- [ ]
- [ ]
- [ ]

SATURDAY

- [ ]
- [ ]
- [ ]
- [ ]
- [ ]
- [ ]
- [ ]

SUNDAY

- [ ]
- [ ]
- [ ]
- [ ]
- [ ]
- [ ]
- [ ]

MOM TIME!

SELF CARE Checklist

SELF CARE LIST

MON:

TUES:

WED:

THUR:

FRI:

SAT:

SUN:

REMINDERS

MY PERSONAL TO-DO LIST:

☐
☐
☐
☐
☐
☐
☐
☐
☐
☐
☐
☐
☐
☐
☐
☐

FROM MOM'S Kitchen

Recipe

PREP TIME:	BAKE TIME:	SERVES:

Ingredients

Directions

FROM MOM'S Kitchen

Recipe

PREP TIME:	BAKE TIME:	SERVES:

Ingredients

Directions

KIDS CHORE Chart

NAME:							

CHORE:	M:	T:	W:	T:	F:	S:	S:

KIDS CHORE Chart

NAME:

CHORE:	M:	T:	W:	T:	F:	S:	S:

KIDS CHORE Chart

NAME:

CHORE:	M:	T:	W:	T:	F:	S:	S:

MY PERSONAL Goals

MY WEEKLY GOALS

MY MONTHLY GOALS

MY YEARLY GOALS

TURN Dreams INTO Reality

TIME FRAME	MY GOALS	STEPS I'LL TAKE
6 MONTHS		
1 YEAR		
2 YEARS		
5 YEARS		

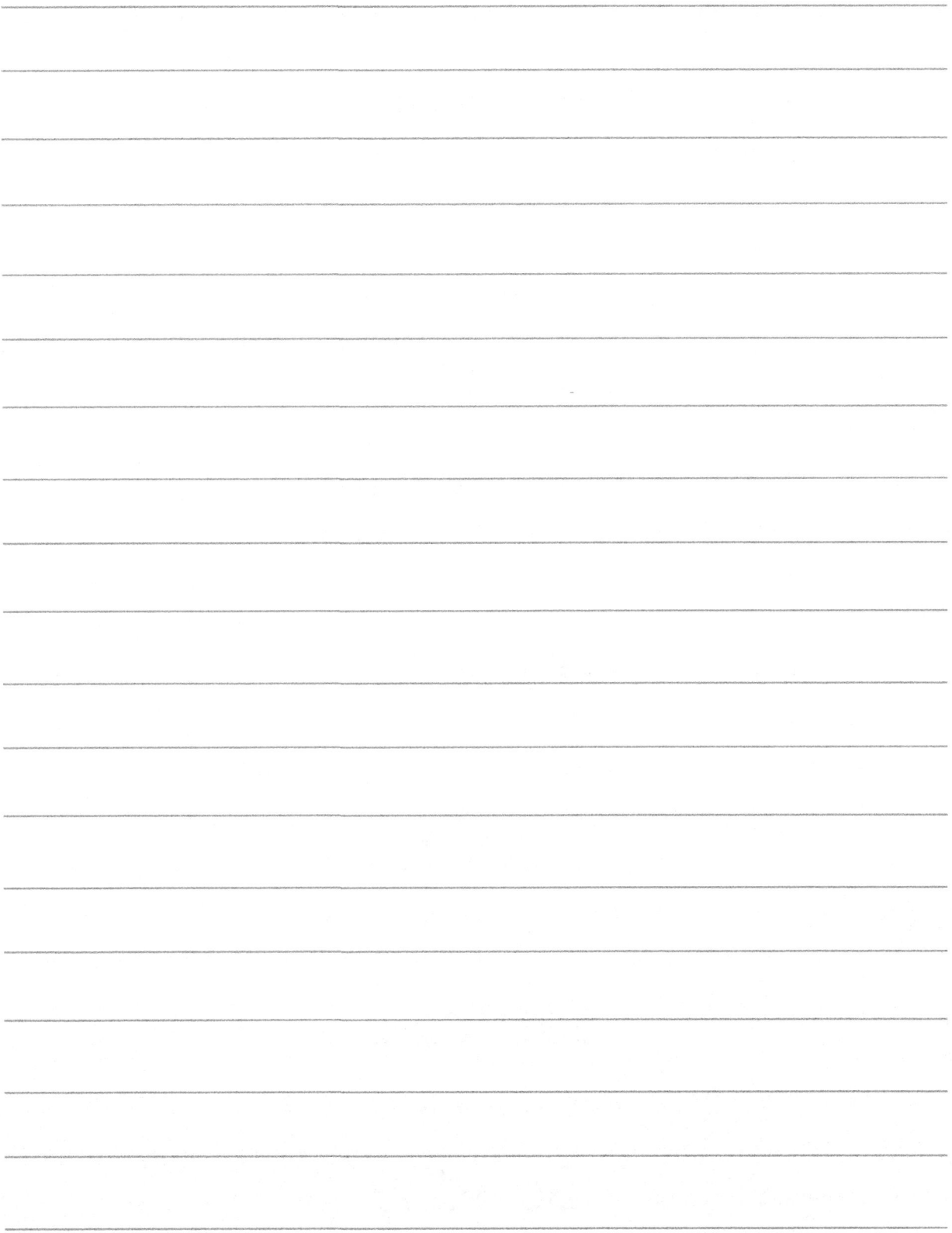

MEALS FOR THE WEEK

Monday

Tuesday

Wednesday

Thursday

Friday

Saturday

Sunday

FAMILY MEAL Planner

WEEK OF:

MEALS	M:	T:	W:	T:	F:	S:	S:
BREAKFAST							
SNACK							
LUNCH							
SNACK							
DINNER							
SNACK							

SHOPPING Checklist

GROCERY **Checklist**

Produce

Meats

Dairy

Frozen

Desserts

Misc.

TO DO Checklist

MONDAY

- [ ]
- [ ]
- [ ]
- [ ]
- [ ]
- [ ]
- [ ]
- [ ]

TUESDAY

- [ ]
- [ ]
- [ ]
- [ ]
- [ ]
- [ ]
- [ ]
- [ ]

WEDNESDAY

- [ ]
- [ ]
- [ ]
- [ ]
- [ ]
- [ ]
- [ ]
- [ ]

THURSDAY

- [ ]
- [ ]
- [ ]
- [ ]
- [ ]
- [ ]
- [ ]
- [ ]

FRIDAY

- [ ]
- [ ]
- [ ]
- [ ]
- [ ]
- [ ]
- [ ]
- [ ]

SATURDAY

- [ ]
- [ ]
- [ ]
- [ ]
- [ ]
- [ ]
- [ ]
- [ ]

SUNDAY

- [ ]
- [ ]
- [ ]
- [ ]
- [ ]
- [ ]
- [ ]
- [ ]

MOM TIME!

HOUSEWORK Checklist

CLEANING

- [ ]
- [ ]
- [ ]
- [ ]
- [ ]
- [ ]
- [ ]

- [ ]
- [ ]
- [ ]
- [ ]
- [ ]
- [ ]
- [ ]

WEEKLY CLEANING TO DO LIST

- [ ]
- [ ]
- [ ]
- [ ]
- [ ]
- [ ]
- [ ]

- [ ]
- [ ]
- [ ]
- [ ]
- [ ]
- [ ]
- [ ]

MONTHLY CLEANING TO DO LIST

- [ ]
- [ ]
- [ ]
- [ ]
- [ ]
- [ ]
- [ ]

- [ ]
- [ ]
- [ ]
- [ ]
- [ ]
- [ ]
- [ ]

WEEKLY TASK Checklist

MONDAY

- [ ]
- [ ]
- [ ]
- [ ]
- [ ]
- [ ]
- [ ]
- [ ]

TUESDAY

- [ ]
- [ ]
- [ ]
- [ ]
- [ ]
- [ ]
- [ ]
- [ ]

WEDNESDAY

- [ ]
- [ ]
- [ ]
- [ ]
- [ ]
- [ ]
- [ ]
- [ ]

THURSDAY

- [ ]
- [ ]
- [ ]
- [ ]
- [ ]
- [ ]
- [ ]
- [ ]

FRIDAY

- [ ]
- [ ]
- [ ]
- [ ]
- [ ]
- [ ]
- [ ]
- [ ]

SATURDAY

- [ ]
- [ ]
- [ ]
- [ ]
- [ ]
- [ ]
- [ ]
- [ ]

SUNDAY

- [ ]
- [ ]
- [ ]
- [ ]
- [ ]
- [ ]
- [ ]
- [ ]

MOM TIME!

SELF CARE Checklist

SELF CARE LIST
MON:
TUES:
WED:
THUR:
FRI:
SAT:
SUN:

MY PERSONAL TO-DO LIST:

☐
☐
☐
☐
☐
☐
☐
☐
☐
☐
☐
☐
☐
☐
☐
☐

REMINDERS

FROM MOM'S Kitchen

Recipe

PREP TIME:	BAKE TIME:	SERVES:

Ingredients

Directions

FROM MOM'S Kitchen

Recipe

PREP TIME:

BAKE TIME:

SERVES:

Ingredients

Directions

KIDS CHORE Chart

NAME:

CHORE:	M:	T:	W:	T:	F:	S:	S:

KIDS CHORE Chart

NAME:

CHORE:	M:	T:	W:	T:	F:	S:	S:

KIDS CHORE Chart

NAME:

CHORE:	M:	T:	W:	T:	F:	S:	S:

MY PERSONAL Goals

MY WEEKLY GOALS

MY MONTHLY GOALS

MY YEARLY GOALS

TURN Dreams INTO Reality

TIME FRAME	MY GOALS	STEPS I'LL TAKE
6 MONTHS		
1 YEAR		
2 YEARS		
5 YEARS		

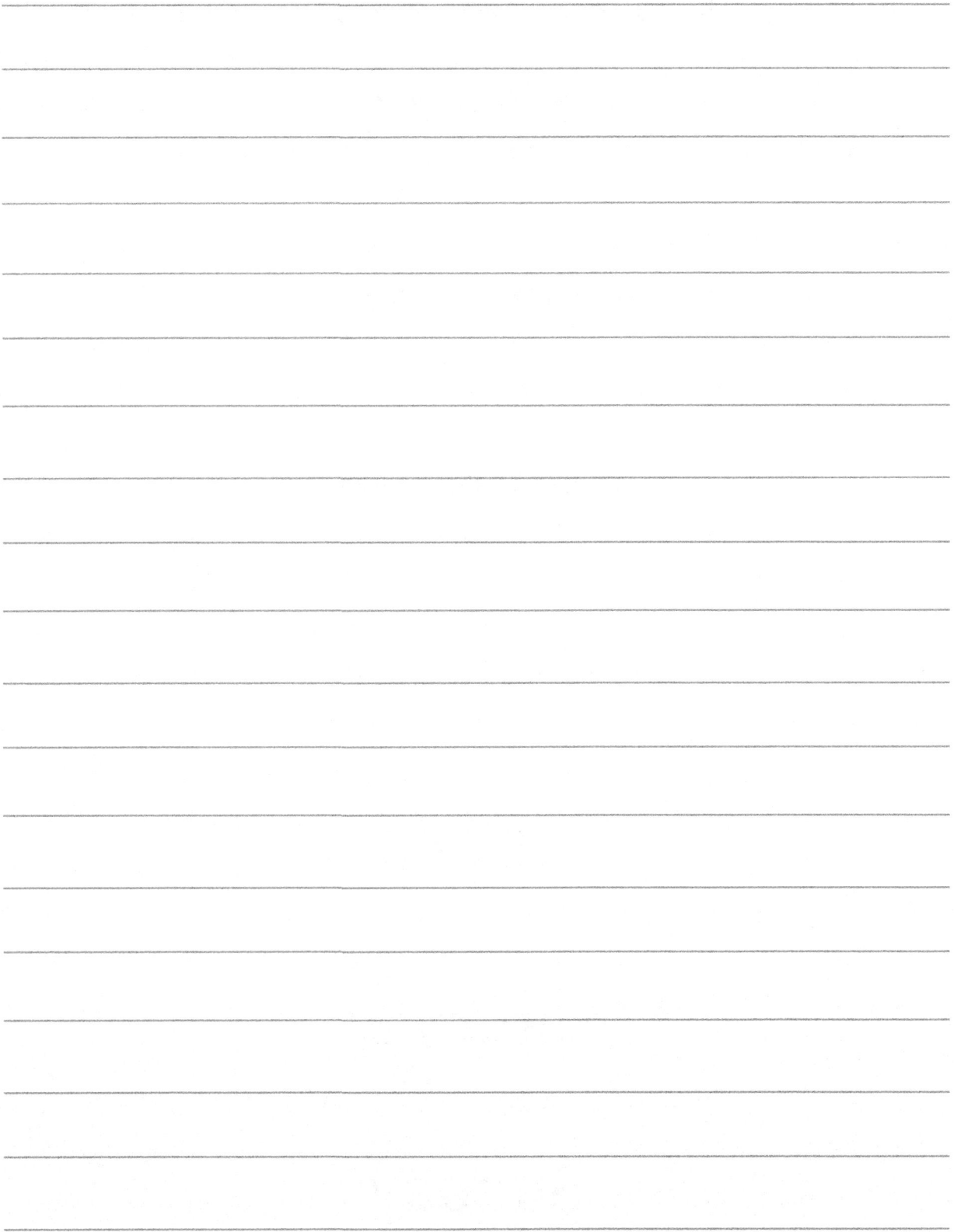

MEALS FOR THE WEEK

Monday

Tuesday

Wednesday

Thursday

Friday

Saturday

Sunday

FAMILY MEAL Planner

WEEK OF: _____

MEALS	M:	T:	W:	T:	F:	S:	S:
BREAKFAST							
SNACK							
LUNCH							
SNACK							
DINNER							
SNACK							

SHOPPING Checklist

GROCERY Checklist

Produce

_____
_____
_____
_____
_____
_____
_____
_____
_____
_____
_____

Meats

_____
_____
_____
_____
_____
_____
_____
_____
_____
_____
_____

Dairy

_____
_____
_____
_____
_____
_____
_____
_____
_____
_____
_____

Frozen

_____
_____
_____
_____
_____
_____
_____
_____

Desserts

_____
_____
_____
_____
_____
_____
_____
_____

Misc.

_____
_____
_____
_____
_____
_____
_____
_____

TO DO Checklist

MONDAY

- [ ]
- [ ]
- [ ]
- [ ]
- [ ]
- [ ]
- [ ]

TUESDAY

- [ ]
- [ ]
- [ ]
- [ ]
- [ ]
- [ ]
- [ ]
- [ ]

WEDNESDAY

- [ ]
- [ ]
- [ ]
- [ ]
- [ ]
- [ ]
- [ ]

THURSDAY

- [ ]
- [ ]
- [ ]
- [ ]
- [ ]
- [ ]
- [ ]
- [ ]

FRIDAY

- [ ]
- [ ]
- [ ]
- [ ]
- [ ]
- [ ]
- [ ]
- [ ]

SATURDAY

- [ ]
- [ ]
- [ ]
- [ ]
- [ ]
- [ ]

SUNDAY

- [ ]
- [ ]
- [ ]
- [ ]
- [ ]
- [ ]
- [ ]

MOM TIME!

HOUSEWORK Checklist

CLEANING

WEEKLY CLEANING TO DO LIST

MONTHLY CLEANING TO DO LIST

WEEKLY TASK Checklist

MONDAY

- [ ]
- [ ]
- [ ]
- [ ]
- [ ]
- [ ]
- [ ]
- [ ]

TUESDAY

- [ ]
- [ ]
- [ ]
- [ ]
- [ ]
- [ ]
- [ ]
- [ ]

WEDNESDAY

- [ ]
- [ ]
- [ ]
- [ ]
- [ ]
- [ ]
- [ ]
- [ ]

THURSDAY

- [ ]
- [ ]
- [ ]
- [ ]
- [ ]
- [ ]
- [ ]
- [ ]

FRIDAY

- [ ]
- [ ]
- [ ]
- [ ]
- [ ]
- [ ]
- [ ]
- [ ]

SATURDAY

- [ ]
- [ ]
- [ ]
- [ ]
- [ ]
- [ ]
- [ ]

SUNDAY

- [ ]
- [ ]
- [ ]
- [ ]
- [ ]
- [ ]
- [ ]
- [ ]

MOM TIME!

SELF CARE Checklist

SELF CARE LIST
MON:
TUES:
WED:
THUR:
FRI:
SAT:
SUN:

MY PERSONAL TO-DO LIST:

☐
☐
☐
☐
☐
☐
☐
☐
☐
☐
☐
☐
☐
☐
☐

REMINDERS

FROM MOM'S Kitchen

Recipe

PREP TIME:	BAKE TIME:	SERVES:

Ingredients

Directions

FROM MOM'S Kitchen

Recipe

PREP TIME:	BAKE TIME:	SERVES:

Ingredients

Directions

KIDS CHORE Chart

NAME:

CHORE:	M:	T:	W:	T:	F:	S:	S:

KIDS CHORE Chart

NAME:

CHORE:	M:	T:	W:	T:	F:	S:	S:

KIDS CHORE Chart

NAME:

CHORE:	M:	T:	W:	T:	F:	S:	S:

MY PERSONAL Goals

MY WEEKLY GOALS

MY MONTHLY GOALS

MY YEARLY GOALS

TURN Dreams INTO Reality

TIME FRAME	MY GOALS	STEPS I'LL TAKE
6 MONTHS		
1 YEAR		
2 YEARS		
5 YEARS		

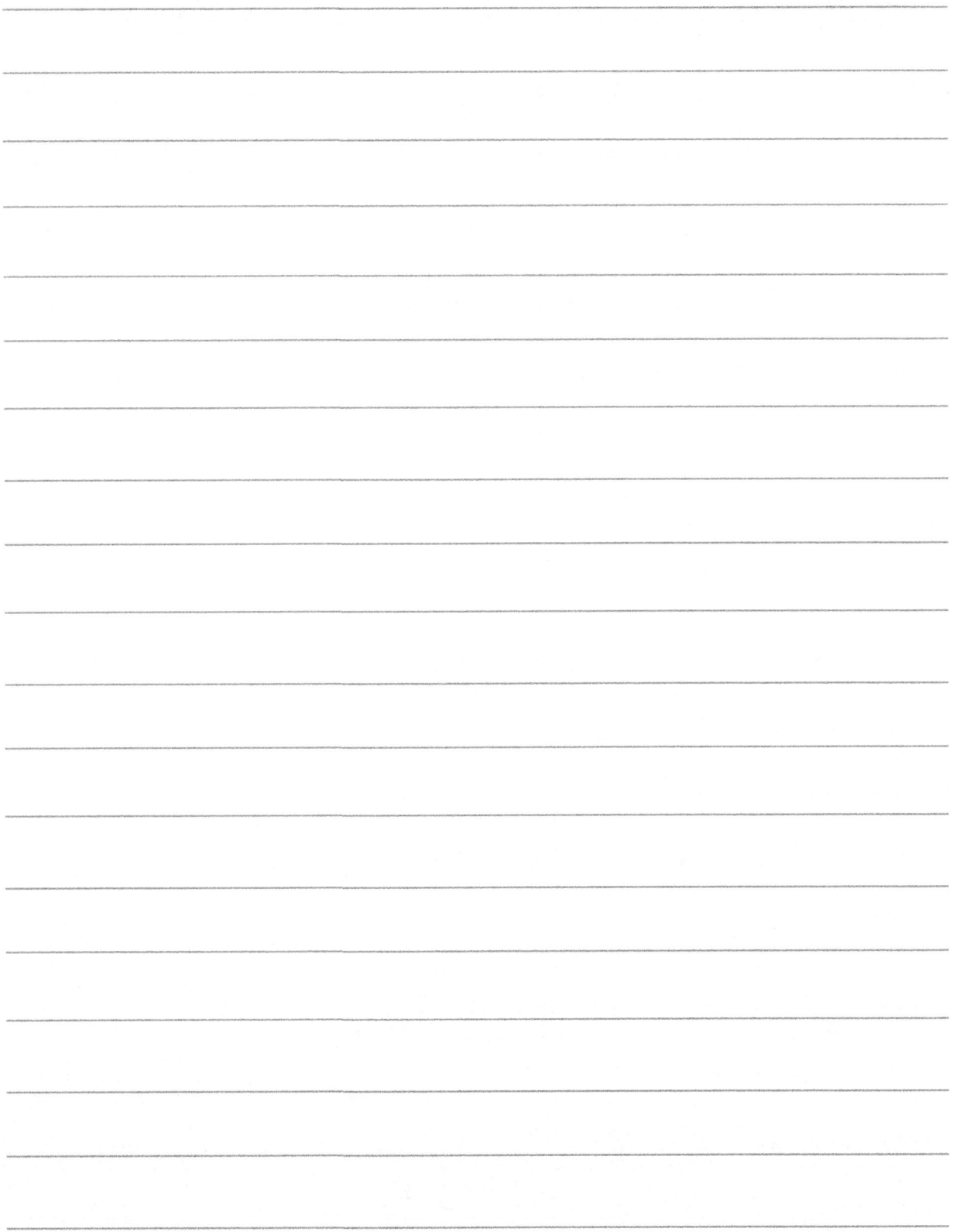

MEALS FOR THE WEEK

Monday

Tuesday

Wednesday

Thursday

Friday

Saturday

Sunday

FAMILY MEAL Planner

WEEK OF:

MEALS	M:	T:	W:	T:	F:	S:	S:
BREAKFAST							
SNACK							
LUNCH							
SNACK							
DINNER							
SNACK							

SHOPPING Checklist

GROCERY Checklist

Produce

Meats

Dairy

Frozen

Desserts

Misc.

TO DO Checklist

MONDAY
- [ ]
- [ ]
- [ ]
- [ ]
- [ ]
- [ ]
- [ ]
- [ ]

TUESDAY
- [ ]
- [ ]
- [ ]
- [ ]
- [ ]
- [ ]
- [ ]
- [ ]

WEDNESDAY
- [ ]
- [ ]
- [ ]
- [ ]
- [ ]
- [ ]
- [ ]
- [ ]

THURSDAY
- [ ]
- [ ]
- [ ]
- [ ]
- [ ]
- [ ]
- [ ]
- [ ]

FRIDAY
- [ ]
- [ ]
- [ ]
- [ ]
- [ ]
- [ ]
- [ ]
- [ ]

SATURDAY
- [ ]
- [ ]
- [ ]
- [ ]
- [ ]
- [ ]
- [ ]
- [ ]

SUNDAY
- [ ]
- [ ]
- [ ]
- [ ]
- [ ]
- [ ]
- [ ]
- [ ]

MOM TIME!

HOUSEWORK Checklist

CLEANING

WEEKLY CLEANING TO DO LIST

MONTHLY CLEANING TO DO LIST

WEEKLY TASK Checklist

MONDAY

- [ ]
- [ ]
- [ ]
- [ ]
- [ ]
- [ ]
- [ ]

TUESDAY

- [ ]
- [ ]
- [ ]
- [ ]
- [ ]
- [ ]
- [ ]

WEDNESDAY

- [ ]
- [ ]
- [ ]
- [ ]
- [ ]
- [ ]
- [ ]

THURSDAY

- [ ]
- [ ]
- [ ]
- [ ]
- [ ]
- [ ]
- [ ]

FRIDAY

- [ ]
- [ ]
- [ ]
- [ ]
- [ ]
- [ ]
- [ ]

SATURDAY

- [ ]
- [ ]
- [ ]
- [ ]
- [ ]
- [ ]
- [ ]

SUNDAY

- [ ]
- [ ]
- [ ]
- [ ]
- [ ]
- [ ]
- [ ]

MOM TIME!

SELF CARE Checklist

SELF CARE LIST
MON:
TUES:
WED:
THUR:
FRI:
SAT:
SUN:

MY PERSONAL TO-DO LIST:

☐
☐
☐
☐
☐
☐
☐
☐
☐
☐
☐
☐
☐
☐
☐

REMINDERS

FROM MOM'S Kitchen

Recipe

PREP TIME:	BAKE TIME:	SERVES:

Ingredients

Directions

FROM MOM'S Kitchen

Recipe

PREP TIME:

BAKE TIME:

SERVES:

Ingredients

Directions

KIDS CHORE Chart

NAME:

CHORE:	M:	T:	W:	T:	F:	S:	S:

KIDS CHORE Chart

NAME:

CHORE:	M:	T:	W:	T:	F:	S:	S:

KIDS CHORE Chart

NAME:

CHORE:	M:	T:	W:	T:	F:	S:	S:

MY PERSONAL Goals

MY WEEKLY GOALS

- ☐
- ☐
- ☐
- ☐
- ☐
- ☐
- ☐
- ☐

MY MONTHLY GOALS

- ☐
- ☐
- ☐
- ☐
- ☐
- ☐
- ☐
- ☐

MY YEARLY GOALS

- ☐
- ☐
- ☐
- ☐
- ☐
- ☐

- ☐
- ☐
- ☐
- ☐
- ☐
- ☐

TURN Dreams INTO Reality

TIME FRAME	MY GOALS	STEPS I'LL TAKE
6 MONTHS		
1 YEAR		
2 YEARS		
5 YEARS		

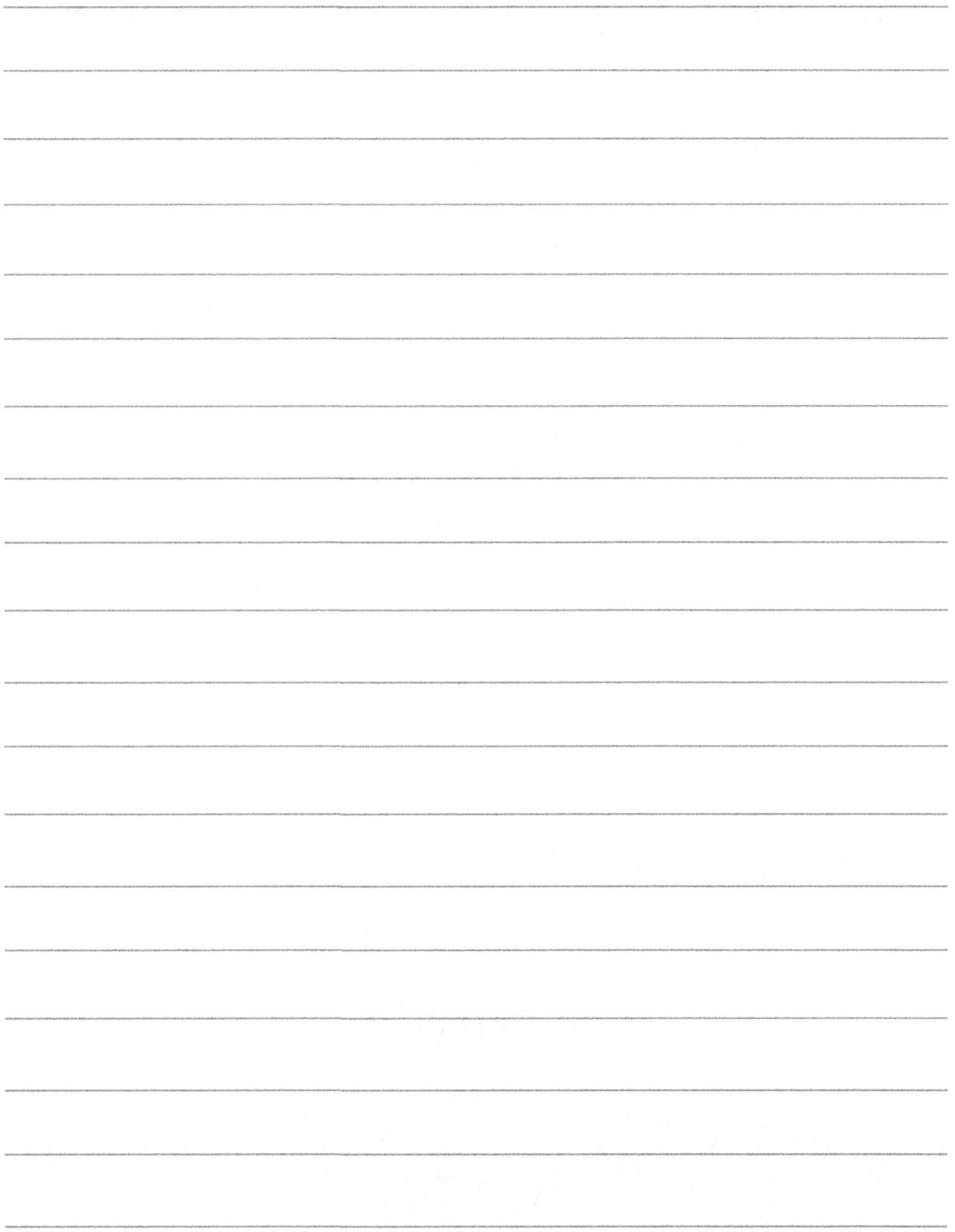

MEALS FOR THE WEEK

Monday

Tuesday

Wednesday

Thursday

Friday

Saturday

Sunday

FAMILY MEAL Planner

WEEK OF:

MEALS	M:	T:	W:	T:	F:	S:	S:
BREAKFAST							
SNACK							
LUNCH							
SNACK							
DINNER							
SNACK							

SHOPPING Checklist

GROCERY Checklist

Produce

Meats

Dairy

Frozen

Desserts

Misc.

TO DO Checklist

MONDAY
- [ ]
- [ ]
- [ ]
- [ ]
- [ ]
- [ ]
- [ ]
- [ ]

TUESDAY
- [ ]
- [ ]
- [ ]
- [ ]
- [ ]
- [ ]
- [ ]
- [ ]

WEDNESDAY
- [ ]
- [ ]
- [ ]
- [ ]
- [ ]
- [ ]
- [ ]
- [ ]

THURSDAY
- [ ]
- [ ]
- [ ]
- [ ]
- [ ]
- [ ]
- [ ]
- [ ]

FRIDAY
- [ ]
- [ ]
- [ ]
- [ ]
- [ ]
- [ ]
- [ ]
- [ ]

SATURDAY
- [ ]
- [ ]
- [ ]
- [ ]
- [ ]
- [ ]
- [ ]
- [ ]

SUNDAY
- [ ]
- [ ]
- [ ]
- [ ]
- [ ]
- [ ]
- [ ]
- [ ]

MOM TIME!

HOUSEWORK Checklist

CLEANING

WEEKLY CLEANING TO DO LIST

MONTHLY CLEANING TO DO LIST

WEEKLY TASK Checklist

MONDAY

- [ ]
- [ ]
- [ ]
- [ ]
- [ ]
- [ ]
- [ ]

TUESDAY

- [ ]
- [ ]
- [ ]
- [ ]
- [ ]
- [ ]
- [ ]

WEDNESDAY

- [ ]
- [ ]
- [ ]
- [ ]
- [ ]
- [ ]
- [ ]

THURSDAY

- [ ]
- [ ]
- [ ]
- [ ]
- [ ]
- [ ]
- [ ]

FRIDAY

- [ ]
- [ ]
- [ ]
- [ ]
- [ ]
- [ ]
- [ ]

SATURDAY

- [ ]
- [ ]
- [ ]
- [ ]
- [ ]
- [ ]
- [ ]

SUNDAY

- [ ]
- [ ]
- [ ]
- [ ]
- [ ]
- [ ]
- [ ]

MOM TIME!

SELF CARE Checklist

SELF CARE LIST
MON:
TUES:
WED:
THUR:
FRI:
SAT:
SUN:

MY PERSONAL TO-DO LIST:

☐
☐
☐
☐
☐
☐
☐
☐
☐
☐
☐
☐
☐
☐
☐

REMINDERS

FROM MOM'S Kitchen

Recipe

PREP TIME:	BAKE TIME:	SERVES:

Ingredients

Directions

FROM MOM'S Kitchen

Recipe

PREP TIME:	BAKE TIME:	SERVES:

Ingredients

Directions

KIDS CHORE Chart

NAME:

CHORE:	M:	T:	W:	T:	F:	S:	S:

KIDS CHORE Chart

NAME:

CHORE:	M:	T:	W:	T:	F:	S:	S:

KIDS CHORE Chart

NAME:

CHORE:	M:	T:	W:	T:	F:	S:	S:

MY PERSONAL Goals

MY WEEKLY GOALS

MY MONTHLY GOALS

MY YEARLY GOALS

TURN Dreams INTO Reality

TIME FRAME	MY GOALS	STEPS I'LL TAKE
6 MONTHS		
1 YEAR		
2 YEARS		
5 YEARS		

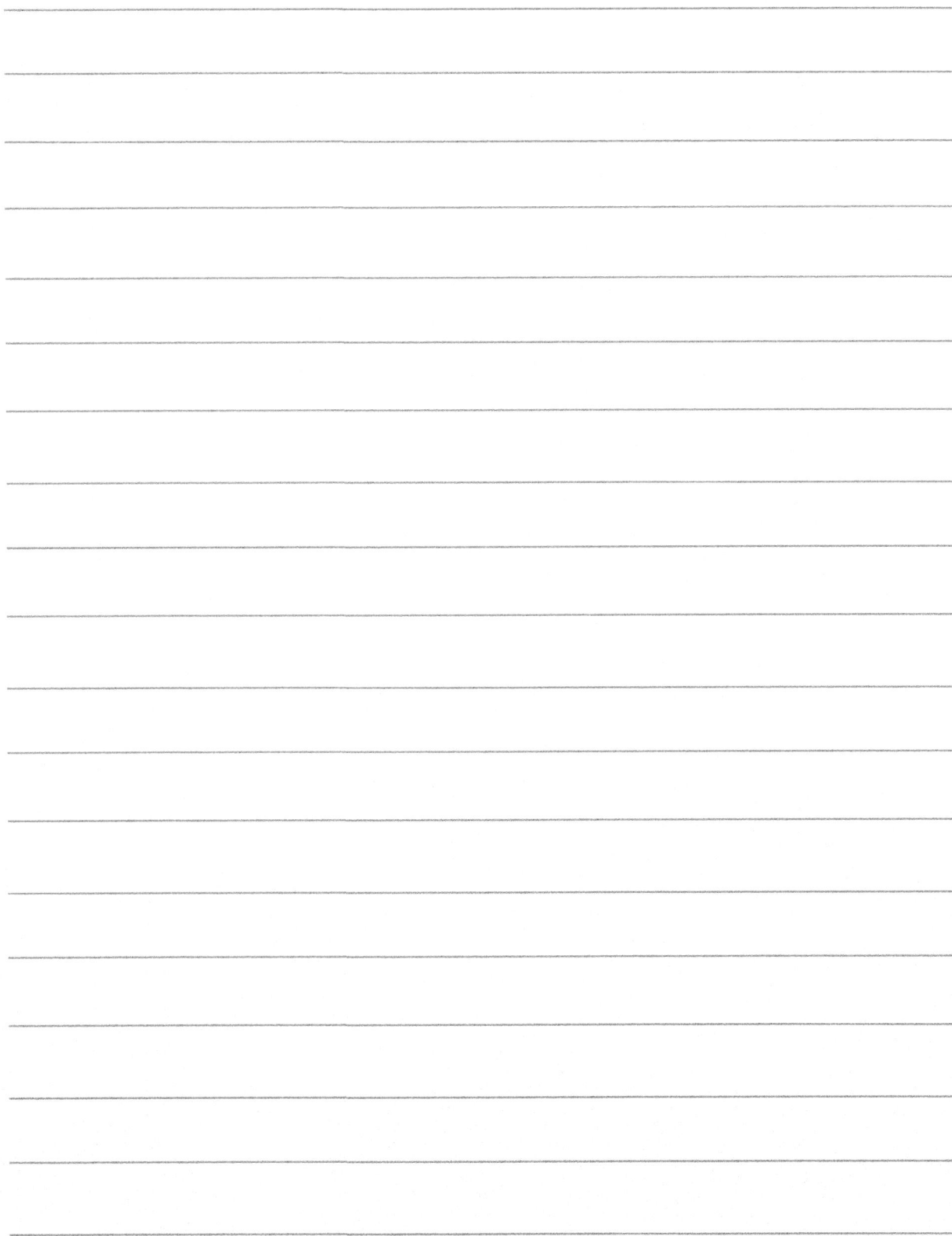

Made in the USA
Las Vegas, NV
15 January 2022

41397717R00116